What Does God Expect?
A Gospel-based Approach to
Christian Conduct

Mark Joseph Young

ISBN: 978-1-989940-48-8
©2005 M. Joseph Young
2nd edition ©2022 Mark Joseph Young
Dimensionfold Publishing

Table of Contents

Introduction

Over the years, many books have been written on Christian conduct, explaining to Christians how we ought to act. These have generally suffered from many of the same faults.

First, most of the books written about how we ought to behave as Christians have a lot more to do with cultural mores and modern standards than with the Gospel of Christ. This leads to many other problems, including that they tend to become obsolete rather quickly. A book that addresses questions of hair styles and clothing and entertainment choices won't be much use when the culture around it changes.

Second, these books tend to distort the Gospel, replacing the freedom in Christ with a modern legalism that is little better than that of the Judaizers who plagued Paul now almost two millennia ago. That is, Paul never preached a message of rules to follow, nor did the other apostles. Rather, they preached that we must love God and each other, and avoid any message that attempts to list the do's and don'ts of pleasing God.

Third, a book that tells you what you should be doing and not doing is little help when you inevitably come to that moment in your life where something in front of you is not covered by the book. Books on conduct cannot possibly cover everything even that is in everyone's life today; to expect them to be able to give definitive answers to the problems of next week, or next year, or the next generation, is asking too much.

This book does not attempt or intend to give you lists of right or wrong conduct. Rather, in approaching the question of Christian conduct, it will present not what the author thinks is right and wrong, nor what some denomination has decreed, nor even some grand list of Biblically-derived rules, but rather a truly Biblical approach to understanding Christian conduct which will make it possible for the reader to find his own way through the moral, ethical, and practical decisions which confront each of us.

On our way to this understanding, we will uncover concepts of Christian guidance, look at the true nature of humility, understand what it is to be the stronger or weaker brother, examine profitable, edifying, and necessary conduct, and more.

Before we reach any of that, though, we must come to understand the Gospel of Christ in a way that most Christians fail to grasp it, not as an introduction to a new code of conduct but as a way of salvation in which what we do does not bring us to it but naturally flows from it.

The translation cited here most often is the UNASB, the Updated New American Standard Bible, the version of my preferred translation currently available from Zondervan. Any text not otherwise marked is from that version.

The Gospel

The Secret

Everybody wants to know the secret.
Everyone is looking for a way.
People tell us how to get to heaven,
But they disagree in what they say.

Some men say sincerity
Will pay the price of liberty,
But people make mistakes when they're sincere.
Some men tell you to believe
Anything you do believe,
But that doesn't seem to be quite clear.

I've waded through the answers.
I've found the one that's true.
So if you'll stop and listen,
I'll pass it on to you.

God expects perfection from your birth until your death.
This is all you really have to do:
Keep your whole life perfect with your every passing breath.
This is what the Lord expects of you.

Keep the ten commandments, the eleventh, and the twelfth.
Love the Lord above all else,
And love your neighbor as yourself,
Show kindness to your enemy,
And give to all abundantly,

Never hate a man, never tell a lie,
Never doubt the truth, never question why,
Always bear the pain, always take the time,
Always keep the law, always stay in line.

Then perhaps you'll make it to his throne.
Then perhaps you'll make it on your own.

But if you've any trouble, there's a better way:
Turn around and give your life to Christ,
And God will touch you with His power,
 and starting from that day
He'll give to you a brand new kind of life.

Yes, if you've any trouble, there's a better way:
Turn around and give your life to Christ,
And God will touch you with His power,
 and starting from that day
He'll give to you a brand new kind of life.

"Are you so foolish? Having begun by the spirit, are you now being perfected by the flesh?" (Galatians 4:3)

Throughout much of the modern world, we preach a "simple" gospel—not an incorrect one, mind, but one that has been reduced to the bare essentials. We can preach it quickly and easily, get people to see and understand what we are saying, and bring them to Christ.

Then, sometime after that, either we try to explain to them that there is more to it than what they heard, or we leave them floundering with little notion of what they should do next. We're a bit like salesmen telling prospective buyers all the wonderful things about the product, and then after we've got the signature on the contract we suggest that the buyer read the small print. The gospel is indeed what God is doing for us, and it is a great thing God has done. However, it is also the most demanding faith in the world, because it does not ask that we perform certain rituals at prescribed times, or that we follow carefully enumerated rules of conduct, but that we give our very lives, the control of our own destinies, to Another. We minimize this in our preaching, because we so desperately want people to be saved that we don't encourage them to count the cost. We say, "If you do something which we are going to call giving your life to Christ, whatever that might mean, God will fulfill your deepest hopes and dreams and make your life wonderful and bring you to heaven in the end." This isn't a lie, exactly; yet it is misleading in its emphasis. We would be more honest if we were to say, "God is ready to make you the person you were made to be, to bring you to the only place where you could possibly be truly happy, as soon as you are willing to give up all of your own hopes and dreams and accept His absolute leadership for your life." We would probably see a lot fewer hands raised to accept that salvation, but at least those who came forward would know what they were buying.

However, because so many of us came to God through that misleading message, we really don't understand what we've begun. So even our preachers and teachers fall into the trap of trying to define what we "should" do in terms that are not much better than legalism. This is nothing new; the church has always had difficulty understanding the ramifications of its own message. Even in the second century we see this confusion. A book surviving from that age, badly misnomered *The Teaching of the Twelve Apostles* (or shortened to *The Didache* by those familiar with its Greek text), illustrates this. In one passage it tells us how important it is that we not be like the Pharisees. They, we are told, fast every Tuesday and Thursday, and we are not to be like them. Since we are not to be like them, we must fast every Wednesday and Friday. This sort of shallow thinking is humorous, but it's no worse than the many variations of rules of Christian conduct being preached from pulpits and presented in books today. The gospel is not about God saving us so that we could adopt a higher standard of conduct. It is about God saving us because we could not possibly live up to His expectations, and giving us an entirely new system for how to live that has nothing to do with rules and regulations.

5

So what is the gospel, really?

Paul wrote his longest single letter, to Romans, solely to lay out in detail exactly what the gospel is. The scope and power of this one epistle cannot be understated. It is the foundation of the work of Augustine, the crucial text in the ministry of Luther, and the inspiration for the theology of Calvin, just to look at the tip of the iceberg. This book cannot fully present all that is in that masterful exposition of the gospel; it is doubtful whether even those giants of the faith fully grasped all that is there. Still, from it we can learn the basics, the most important points in our salvation, the true gospel as Paul preached it.

In the middle of the first chapter, Paul begins showing that everyone is condemned by the Law of God. Beginning at 1:18, he speaks of the one sin which all sinners share, as they look for new ways to offend: sinners have decided that they are a law unto themselves, and can themselves decide what they will do. Since they have taken for themselves the right to decide right and wrong, denying God the right to tell them what is right and wrong, they have been sucked into a vortex of immorality upon depravity upon corruption. In 1:32 Paul says, "and although they know the ordinance of God, that those who practice such things are worthy of death, they not only do the same, but also give hearty approval to those who practice them." That is, they cannot help but know that God says these things are wrong, but even if they don't do them, they still sin when they say it's perfectly all right for others to do them, because the sin isn't so much what they do, but that they declare themselves the judge of what is permitted, a position that belongs only to God.

Once we see that the right to judge right and wrong belongs solely to God, we understand why, in chapter 2, Paul attacks the good people. His age, as ours, was filled with moralists, people who were decrying the evils of society and announcing a moral high ground. However, Paul says, when you raise a standard and declare that everyone must act in accordance with your moral code, you have admitted that there is a code, and taken it upon yourself to be the judge. You are doing exactly the same thing as those you condemn. You are putting yourself in the place of God, deciding that you have the power to decide right and wrong. Only God has that authority, and you sin if you try to take that place and preach to people how they ought to act. Not only that, but by admitting that there's an appropriate standard of conduct, you are without excuse when you fail to live up to God's standard of conduct in every particular—that standard which He delivered to Moses, to Israel, with all of its regulations concerning eating and washing and making sacrifices as well as the rules we imagine are the big ones. No, if there's any standard of conduct, it's God's standard; anyone who preaches a different standard is putting himself in the place of God. He is just as bad as the one who throws himself into the sensual debauchery of the world, because both are committing the one sin that really matters: they are replacing the judgment of God with their own.

Christian preachers, though, would argue that we have the Word of God, we have the Scripture, and we are in a position to tell the world not what we think but what God thinks. Paul had words for us as well. In his age, there was a group that had the commandments of God, who quite reasonably could declare that they knew what God demanded of us. He addresses them starting in 2:17; they are the Jewish moralists. Just because they were Jewish, not Christian, does not mean that this passage does not address us. Paul is talking to those who would use the Law of God as the standard by which to judge the conduct of the world, and of the people of the world. He challenges us to consider whether we keep the Law, fully and in every respect, or whether we ourselves might be guilty of infringing the very commandments (perhaps in other ways) which we would enforce. It is no good, he says, to preach the law if you don't keep it. What, though, if you do? What if you can say, as Paul said of himself, "according to the righteousness which is in the Law, found blameless"? (Philippians 3:6b) These do not escape Paul's eye. Starting in Romans 3:9 he marshals an array

7

of scripture which condemns everyone. "There is none righteous....All have turned aside....Their throat is an open grave....Their feet are swift to shed blood....And the path of peace they have not known. There is no fear of God before their eyes." These words were written in the Law, Paul tells us. They aren't addressed to others. They are addressed to us, to those who know and follow the Law. The Bible clearly states "by works of the Law no flesh will be justified in His sight" (Romans 3:20), and it means that godliness is not about obeying some set of rules. "But now apart from the Law the righteousness of God has been manifested" (Romans 3:21)— that is, we have been made righteous, put right with God and declared holy, without any reference to what we do. "For we maintain that a man is justified by faith apart from works of the Law." (Romans 3:28).

To truly understand the gospel, you must see that there are two systems, completely independent of each other. There is not one system that has been adapted by another. There are two distinct systems. One system is called Law, and is about doing the right thing all the time. The other system is called Grace, and is about loving God and being loved by Him. Grace is not about adapting the Law down to something we can do. It's about forgetting about Law entirely and coming under a new system. We are "not under law, but under grace." (Romans 6:14 and 6:15) Not one fragment of the Law has been revoked. "Do we then nullify the Law through faith? May it never be! On the contrary, we establish the Law." (Romans 3:31) The Law will stand immutable throughout the ages. It just doesn't apply to us at all, because we are under the new system.

For a brief time I lived in the North Shore area outside Boston; hence I sometimes pick on Boston in my illustrations. If you live there, forgive me. I'm going to pick on Boston in this illustration. Let us suppose that there is a law in Boston that requires all men to shave their heads. To have more hair on your head than Yul Brynner or Telly Savalas or Michael Jordan is to break the law in Boston. It might not surprise you to learn that I am not in compliance with that law. I have a full head of hair, and then some. Clearly I have violated that law. However, I am not guilty. I am not guilty because of jurisdiction. The laws of Boston apply to people who are in Boston, and not to people outside of Boston. I am writing this from New Jersey, and other than that brief stay during college I have lived my life in various places in this state. The laws of Boston do not apply to me because I am outside their jurisdiction. I can wear my hair however I wish.

In the same way, I am not under Law but under Grace. It is a jurisdictional matter. The Law does not apply to me at all; grace applies to me.

How did we come to escape the jurisdiction of Law, and to be under the jurisdiction of Grace? That's easy. We died. You see, "one died for all, therefore all died" (I Corinthians 5:14); "all of us who have been baptized into Christ Jesus have been baptized into His death....we have become united with Him in the likeness of His death....our old self was crucified with Him." (Romans 6:3, 5, 6) As Paul further explains, "the law has jurisdiction over a person as long as he lives....you also were made to die to the Law through the body of Christ....we have been released from the Law, having died to that by which we were bound." (Romans 7:1, 4, 6) We were part of this world, trapped by sin and under the condemnation of the Law of God, but Jesus saved us, pulling us out of this world and starting our new lives as new creatures, part of the new creation, in which the Grace of God is the system.

All of this is to say that those rules and regulations are not part of our faith. Rather, we live by a faith in God that is free from any rules or regulations. Perhaps an illustration will help.

There remains one prominent royal family in the western world, someone whom English-speaking people admire greatly, the Kings, or currently the Queen, of England. They have a code of courtesy and conduct to which they at least give lip service (even if some have failed to adhere to this); to be a member of the royal household is to have an obligation to act in certain ways deemed appropriate. However, if one of our young princes were to fail to act in an appropriate manner, that would not cause him to cease to be a member of the royal family. He is a member of the royal family, without regard for his conduct. Similarly, no one in England can walk up to Buckingham Palace and declare that having kept all of the rules of conduct letter perfect throughout their lives they wish to be admitted to the palace as part of the royal family. Keeping the standards of the family does not make you a royal, just as failing to keep those standards will not expel you. One becomes a member of the royal family by one of three paths. You can be born into the family; you can marry into the family; you can be adopted. It is these three concepts—the New Birth, the Bride of the Lamb, and the Adoption as Sons—which the New Testament uses as its analogies for what it is to be saved. No amount of doing good can gain admittance for you; no failure to do good can cause you to be expelled. Grace will always be sufficient to cover our transgressions.

Then why do good at all? As Paul challenges, "Are we to continue in sin that grace may increase?" (Romans 6:1) He answers that briefly when he asks it. "How shall we who died to sin still live in it? (Romans 6:2), but there is much more to this answer than just those few words. How do we recognize sin, if we don't have law? If what we do doesn't matter to our salvation, why should we be concerned about what we do? If Christ truly has set us free, doesn't that mean we can do whatever we want? In a sense, much of the rest of this book is about that. The next chapter, though, is particularly about it.

The Two Commandments

Jesus walked the streets of Jerusalem in an age during which there were many factions, what we might label denominations of Jews who each believed the scriptures but interpreted them in very different ways. As Jesus was recognized by the people as someone sent from God, these factions often would question Him, hoping that He would lend credibility to their positions or, in the process of attempting to discredit them, would discredit Himself. He frequently presented answers to them which showed how shallow their questions were.

On one of those occasions, the Pharisees attempted to trap Him into picking a "most important" commandment; He rose to the occasion, though, and we read in Matthew 22:37-40, "'You shall love the Lord your God with all your heart, and with all your soul, and with all your mind.' This is the great and foremost commandment. The second is like it, 'You shall love your neighbor as yourself.' On these two commandments depend the whole Law and the Prophets."

The depth of this cannot be fathomed. Augustine, when asked about the rules of conduct demanded by the Gospel, described them as "Love God, and do as you please." The Apostle John, writing to an unidentified church near the end of his life, wrote, "Now I ask you, lady, not as though I were writing to you a new commandment, but the one which we have had from the beginning, that we love one another." (II John 5) Twice Jesus gave that commandment, "that you love one another, even as I have loved you" (John 13:34); "that you love one another, just as I have loved you" (John 15:12). The standard of conduct in the gospel isn't rules, do's and don'ts. It's love for God and for each other. Everything we do stems from love.

However, it stems from proper understanding as well.

11

It is easy to hurt someone very badly, or to fall into terribly grievous sin, in the name of loving someone. It happens because we fail to understand the nature of the world in which we are living, and so we come to believe that some things are good which are actually quite harmful to ourselves and to others.

The young Doctor Sigmund Freud was introduced to a wonder drug of his age, a chemical that had all sorts of marvelous beneficial properties. It enhanced mental clarity, increased perception, and seemed to improve intelligence. It was being used experimentally to relieve morphine addiction. He embraced this, using it himself and encouraging others to use it as well. Among these was his fiancée, Martha Bernays. Unfortunately, the drug, cocaine, proved horribly addictive; they had a great deal of trouble escaping it.

It is easy to see in this case how someone might think that what he was encouraging was a good thing. Freud knew all that was known about the relatively new wonder drug, and used it himself. He wanted his fiancée to have the benefits of this marvelous modern medical miracle. One can imagine him quite honestly saying through tears, "I didn't know; I didn't know." Yet what he didn't know, what he didn't understand about the world, caused both him and his wife great harm, despite his best intentions, even love, toward her.

Some people do give drugs to their loved ones out of a misguided desire to share what they have found. Perhaps some of them actually don't know that these things can kill; some certainly have that sense of immortality found in so many young people, that sense that death is for other people, but as heroes of our own stories we are immune. Some see the perceived benefits of the drugs as outweighing the dangers and costs, for whatever reason. This, though, is a small portion of the damage done by people who act out of love based on faulty knowledge. A great deal of damage is done by giving and taking advice which is not Biblically sound. People are told that they should

12

leave their spouses because it will better for the spouse, that if they truly loved that person they would leave them. We are told that sexual relationships which are not marital relationships are good things, as long as everyone involved is enjoying it. Violence and aggression are encouraged at times when they are inappropriate. There are many things which people are persuaded (or sometimes deluded) into thinking they are doing because of love which are actually the worst things that they could do for the ones they love, or for themselves.

This is why Paul prays for the Philippians, "that your love may abound still more and more in real knowledge and all discernment, so that you may approve the things that are excellent in order to be sincere and blameless until the day of Christ; having been filled with the fruit of righteousness which comes through Jesus Christ, to the glory and praise of God." (Philippians 1:9-11) It is not enough that we love others; we must understand how to show that love to others. We cannot always do what they would have us do, nor what we would want to do; we must do what is best for them.

I have a number of close friends who are nurses. They have sometimes spoken of patients in the intensive care unit who are in great pain, and require morphine to relieve them. The use of morphine is a very tricky thing. The longer a patient uses it, the less effective it is altogether. Once it is no longer needed for pain, it must be reduced gradually to prevent withdrawal. Dosages which are higher than necessary can be fatal. However, it relieves pain and permits patients to sleep. It is a valuable, if dangerous, medication. Still, you can't just give it to patients because they want it. A doctor must determine that they need it, and how much they should be allowed to have. Every nurse wants to give the patient enough to stop the pain, but at the same time recognizes that it must be controlled, limited. To exceed the dose might make the patient feel much better, but in the long run it's going to harm the patient far more than it helps. So the patient might want more, and the nurse might wish to give more out of sympathy for the patient, but knowledge tells us that doing so will do more harm than good. Love, in this case, tempered by real knowledge and all discernment, tells us to give the patient the morphine he needs, not the morphine he may want, and not the morphine we may wish to give.

This is where Law becomes important to us. We are not under law, and we must never imagine that we please God by keeping rules. Rather, we please God by expressing our love for Him and for others through actions which He finds pleasing. The Law then becomes a picture of that which God finds pleasing. As we look at it, we see what He required, and we begin to understand what He is like through it. We see that God commanded us not to kill, and we understand that killing is quite evidently a very hurtful thing; so we decide not to kill, not because we have a rule that says we should not, but because we know that our God is pained by man's choice to hurt each other instead of caring for each other. We love God; therefore we choose to do that which pleases Him.

Many times the Bible relates our relationship with God to a marriage, in both directions: we understand our relationship with God because it is like a marriage, and we understand marriage because it is like our relationship with God. We, however, live in an age of broken relationships, and for many people the images of good relationships lack meaning. There are sons who hate their fathers and fathers who do not care for their sons, and so to many the image of the love of a father for his son or a son for his father does not convey anything of value. There are broken homes and broken marriages which do not reflect anything good (and I would not by this mean that any marriage perfectly reflects the love between Christ and the Church, but only that some do so better than others). Still, nearly all of us have at some time had a genuine feeling of love for someone else. It is this love which should be in our relationships that best shows how we act.

When you are in love, or when you have a genuine love for a parent or child or friend, you want to be pleasing to the beloved. This means you will do two things.

First, you will try to determine what it is that that person wants, desires, and expects from you. You will spend time with him, pay attention to his words, actions, and reactions to things around him. You will ask his other friends what they have discovered about him. You will try to discover how you can please him. You will talk to him, listen to him, reveal yourself to him, and discover him. In every way, you will try to get to know this person that you love.

Second, you will try to be the person whom that person could love. You will do things for him which he will find pleasing. You will act in ways that he will respect and admire. As you discover what he wants you to be, you will become that, so that you will in every way be the person he can love.

In life, the process is imperfect. There are ways in which we cannot be someone else. Yet there are aspects of who we are and what we do that we are able to change, and so we can see how the process works.

With God, the same process is occurring. Because we love Him (and look at all He has done for us, how much we can love Him!) we want to know Him, to discover as much about Him as we can. We read His words, see what He has done in the past, understand what hurts Him and what He admires and expects. We share what we have discovered with others who also love Him, and learn from them what they have discovered—never as rules to follow, but as insights from which we, too, can learn. As we learn who He is, we naturally try to become the kind of people He wants us to be. He won't love us the less if we don't, but because we love Him, we have the desire to be pleasing to Him, perhaps to make Him proud of us.

In this, we have help. Our efforts to act in a manner pleasing to God are supported by God Himself, within us. So that which works to change us in our natural relationships works even better to change us in our spiritual relationship, as God enhances those desires and those efforts through His Spirit within us.

From this flows all Christian conduct. "We love, because He first loved us....and this is the commandment we have from Him, that the one who loves God should love his brother also." (I John 4:19, 21) As we express that love, we are pleasing to God. To express it aright, though, we must understand aright.

Renewing Your Mind

Parable of the Boiler

Let us suppose for the moment that you are in my evening class, and I have just arrived. We're going to get down to business in just a moment, I say, but first I have something I found interesting, which I thought you might appreciate. I have been studying the heat in this old building, and it's badly in need of replacing. One of these days, you know, it's going to go. In fact, I got a friend of mine in here to look at it, and together we pulled together some numbers on metal stress, R-factors, wind chill, some other stuff, and made a projection. According to these numbers, as soon as the outside temperature reaches twenty degrees Farenheit, that boiler is going to explode—it will probably take half the building with it.

I don't imagine that you would believe so wild a notion just because I said so. I may be smart, but this is hardly my field. Yet suppose you can see that I'm laying out diagrams and test results and pages of calculations, all spread out on a table in the classroom, and as you look over the numbers it's very persuasive. You remembered that just before you got out of your car to come inside, the DJ on the radio said that it was 22 degrees downtown, and was expected to fall into single digits before midnight. The way you see it, if I'm right, the boiler will blow up within the hour. Meanwhile, the numbers have convinced you. You now believe that the boiler will explode at any minute. So you say to me, "I see that. I believe that we're going to have an explosion tonight, right here. It will probably take out half the building. Can I get you a cup of coffee before we get started?"

You probably don't say that. You only say that if you are assenting to an interesting theory. If you believe all that I just said, you turn down the thermostat, get out of the building—in essence, you run for your life! (It's very nice of you to offer to stay, but I assure you that if I believe what I just told you, I'm not holding the class here anyway.)

Faith demands action. I have often said, "Theology is everything." What I mean by that is, in the final analysis, what you really believe will control what you actually do. People don't do things which kill them—whether so obvious things as smoking, or those sins which eat away at the soul and destroy us from the inside—we don't do things which kill us because we want to die. We do them because, whatever we may say we believe, we don't really believe that they are dangerous. The person who has an affair, gets an abortion, steals from the company, deceives a friend, cheats on taxes, or murders thirty-seven people in a twelve-state shooting spree doesn't really believe that it's bad for him when he does it—or maybe not ever. Believing that there are negative consequences to our actions is the ultimate deterrent to them. Believing that there are positive consequences to our actions is the ultimate incentive. What we do directly springs from what we truly believe. That's why you are known by your works: because, although you can plaster on a veneer of goodness as easily as you can fake a cold heart, ultimately you will act by what you think. That is why faith requires content; that is why you are "transformed by the renewing of your mind" (Romans 12:2). That is why repentance—metanoia in the Greek—means "to change your thinking". Once you understood the world one way. Now you must learn to understand all things as they really are, for if you truly understand the way everything is, and if you truly believe that things are as God says they are, then you will always do the right thing.

The Word of God is filled with passing comments about the importance of the Word of God. We are to meditate on it, let it dwell in us, study it, teach it—in all ways we are to be immersed in the Word. Parallel to this, it teaches us that our minds, our thoughts, are important. We are to take every thought captive, to be transformed by the renewing of our minds, to change our thinking. These two threads are part of the

18

same concept. We renew our minds by meditating on scripture. As our thoughts change, our perceptions of the world change, and we act differently.

Christian conduct comes from the love we have for God and each other, from the new creation into which we are growing, from the Holy Spirit within us, and from the changes God works in us. There is a sense in which these are individual things; there is another sense in which they are all the same thing. We are changing into new Spirit-filled creatures whose existence is defined by the love we have for God. How do we become these new creatures? As with most things in our Christian life, there is a sense in which it has happened, and a sense in which it will happen, but also a sense in which it is happening now. That is, we are already new creatures, yet when Jesus returns we will be transformed. In the interim, we are being changed from the old creature who lived in the old world to the new creature who lives in the new world. That present transformation happens as our minds are filled with a better understanding of Him, through His word.

In II Corinthians 3:18, Paul speaks of us "beholding as in a mirror the glory of the Lord....being transformed into the same image." He has already spoken to the Corinthians about seeing God "in a mirror dimly", where he explains that as "now I know in part." (I Corinthians 13:12) I don't think it's pushing this too far to say that we see Him, not completely or perfectly but truly and wonderfully, in the words of scripture. Here we find painted for us the image of who God is, what He is like. As we turn to the Bible and read it, study it, memorize and meditate upon it, we see Him.

Then that word within us, empowered by the Holy Spirit, changes us, making us what we should be.

When I started college, I imagined myself one of the "spiritual" people. I had been reading the Bible as long as I could remember, and had been a Christian for a substantial portion of my life. I had won New York's NBC Radio Youth Bible quiz at thirteen, been involved in music ministry for a couple of years, and had read the Bible through in more than one translation. Now I was in a Bible college, and counted myself "spiritual". Indeed, there were students who looked up to me, or who at least attempted to hide their bad habits when I was around because in some way my presence made them feel uncomfortable. However, within a couple of weeks I realized that there were others there who were in some intangible way more spiritual than I. They radiated a warmth, a humility, and an inner power that were nothing like what I knew.

Even then I had the spirit of a teacher, and as a result I made the mistake of a teacher. I assumed that they had discovered some truth, some special secret about the Christian life that I had not yet found, had not read in any of the many books I had read. I thought that if I just knew this thing, whatever it was, I would be like them, more "spiritual" in that intangible way. They knew something I didn't.

Eventually I decided it was more important that I find out what I needed to know to advance to this higher level than to pretend to be more than I was. I caught up with one of these more spiritual people when he was walking alone, and asked him to tell me the secret. There was no secret, he said. He had no idea what I wanted to know. All he knew was to spend time in the Word of God and prayer.

I was certain he was mistaken. Somehow he didn't know what he knew, he couldn't tell me (I would never have imagined that he would have hidden it intentionally). Over the years that followed, however, I discovered that he was correct. He had told me the truth. Growth in God comes from our immersion in scripture and prayer.

I still am not the sort of person who exudes that sort of spirituality. I have learned that this is not who God made me to be. I am a teacher, and I will always be more focused on understanding and explaining truth than anything else in this life. Still, I have also grown much in those times when I was able to focus on these basics. I also am no prayer warrior. God calls some to change the world through their prayers, to call upon Him and see Him move in the world. He has empowered me to change the world in a different way, through helping others understand the truth. For me, it is much more the time spent in the Word that changes me. However, prayer and worship are still part of that process. The point in coming to the Word is coming to God, seeing Him reflected within it. It is by coming to God that we are changed, and we come to God through prayer, through worship, and through scripture. We need all of these things in some measure, but each of us benefits from them in different amounts, and will strike a different balance in them. My point of balance is heavily toward scripture; thus I will say only a few words about prayer and worship, and then focus on what I know best.

God wants us to come to Him in prayer. You will hear many sermons in your life telling you how to pray, and sometimes they will seem to contradict each other. Jesus gave us a prayer, a model for how we should pray, but we cannot agree among ourselves how to use the model. This much is clear: God wants us to ask Him for things. He wants us to ask Him to do the things He wants to do, and He wants us to ask Him to care for our needs. He also wants us to thank Him for what He has done. It is important to keep in mind that He is always working on our behalf. He gives us the good things we have. Even in the bad times there are good things, and they come from His hand. We need to be mindful of this, and to thank Him for whatever we have received. For one thing, this reminds us that it does come from Him, even if we had to work for it. More importantly, it keeps us mindful that we are dependent on Him for all things, and cannot do it ourselves. Above all, prayer is about talking to God. God wants us to be comfortable talking to Him. We are going to be spending a long time in His presence, and we really ought to get used to it now. When you pray, talk to God in your natural language, expressing your real thoughts, feelings, and concerns. You aren't going to surprise Him, and if what you feel would offend Him, you probably need to talk to Him about why you feel that way and what can be done about it.

Worship is the process of declaring the worth of God. I tend to sing songs, but I also worship Him in prayer. Think about all that God is, and allow that to overwhelm you. Then speak from your heart about the wonder.

As to scripture, there are many ways you can immerse yourself in this. I hope that over the years you will try all of these, and more, as each will help.

We live in an age in which it is easy to hear the word. The Bible is published on tape, and many people buy these tapes to listen to them as they drive or work or are otherwise occupied. There are also Bible teachers who produce tapes in which they explain the scriptures. Such extended exposure can be wonderfully helpful. I have spent many hours listening to some excellent teaching tapes, until I could repeat portions of them and use them in my own teaching. There is much that can be learned this way. I only hesitate to encourage this because it is so easy. It's not that you shouldn't also do the easy thing, but that you should not expect the easy thing to replace the more difficult. Yes, you should listen to the Word read, and the Word taught and explained, but if you can read, you should read the Word—and if you can study, you should study it. Hearing the Word is wonderful, but unless that is all you can do, you should do much more.

However you approach your time with God, you will want to do it regularly, in some sense of that word. That is, you may wish to set aside half an hour each day, or you may find that it fits your life better to commit three to four hours on Saturday afternoon. For some people, rising early enables them to get a better start on their day, while others find that they accomplish more if they set this time just before bed. People with very structured schedules often find that their lunch break is the ideal moment to get alone with God (and while this may sound unusual, it was people spending their lunch time praying together which started one of America's Great Awakenings). During the course of your life, you will probably find that different times work better at different times. The point is to be committed to something that keeps you involved. If you decide that you will spend time with God when you get a moment, you will not find that moment, at least not very often.

Don't misunderstand. It is perfectly possible to grow in God without some regular schedule of time devoted to Him. People with very erratic schedules may not be able to specify a time that appears regular to others. Shift workers might not have one time when they are always awake; over the road truckers might live lives almost completely disconnected from day and night. As long as you take the time to be alone with God in some way, when that is doesn't matter. The reason for setting it up on some kind of schedule is to make it a priority, and so ensure that it doesn't fall by the wayside. There will be times in your life during which a "spare moment" seems an impossible thing; yet there is always enough time for God if it is managed properly. Scheduling this time is a way of ensuring that it happens. Doing it as spare moments will certainly give you all the same benefits spiritually, but it will be harder to maintain consistently over the months, over the years, through the changes that life will inevitably bring.

There is no sin in changing the schedule. If you normally have your prayer time on Saturday mornings, but you've been invited to a wedding one weekend, you can shift it to Friday night or Sunday afternoon. God isn't going to be angry if you skip it once in a while. This isn't about doing something that will please God; it's about doing something that will benefit you and help you learn to please Him better. Like a good exercise program, regular practice is better than sporadic bingeing, but any is better than none.

A word should be said about place. It is best if you can find a place that is quiet and private. You don't want distractions. However, you may wish to sing, or to pray loudly or talk aloud to God during your time with Him. A disused room at work, the solitude of your car, a church sanctuary open during the day, a private place at home are all good choices. However, the ideal location might not present itself. God is not concerned with where you are when you call on him. A booth in a fast food restaurant, or a park bench, or a seat on the train, an empty Laundromat in the middle of the night or even a bathroom, can each be an acceptable place to turn to God. It is good to have a place where you are comfortable; it is better to come to God in awkward places than to fail to take the time because you can't find the place.

Also, if one day your ideal place is not available, settle for another place. God certainly isn't going to wonder where you are.

How, then, do you study scripture? How do you make the Word of God part of you? The answer to that is simple: any and every way you can. Here are some ways.

I have always been a fan of what has been called "microstudy". This approach to scripture is built around squeezing every thought out of every word, looking at the Bible sentence by sentence, verse by verse, phrase by phrase, to find out what each part means. You will see microstudy reflected in the pages of this book and other books, places in which the author or the teacher takes each word of a verse and draws from it what it means and how it fits with the other words around it, slowly building the meaning of the whole from that of the parts. The material on humility, later in this book, was developed from just this sort of study, as one verse in Philemon was carefully examined over several days until I understood it.

Microstudy works well with memorization and meditation. In a sense, these are forms of microstudy.

You will find that there are verses in the Bible that you want to remember. This is a good way to start a memorization program; it will be easier to memorize verses you want to know It is helpful to memorize the address with the verse, that is, to know the book and chapter and verse numbers for each verse you memorize; however, the verse numbers are not part of scripture, they are only a way to locate scripture. Eventually you will find it valuable to memorize in a systematic fashion, learning longer passages verse by verse. In this way some have committed to memory at least a few of the shorter books of the Bible, plus chapters and longer passages from other books. It can be done, and done easily, if you choose to do it. If you memorize one verse of scripture each day, by repeating it throughout the day, perhaps by reading it from a card in your pocket or a sign on your desk or a note on your dash, and you repeat the verses you have learned recently, these passages will remain with you. I don't say that in ten years you will be able still to recite them, but you will know them in a way that cannot be taken from you.

Memorization is the beginning of meditation. Meditation is like chewing the cud. You bring back to your mind what you have stored there, and examine it again, looking for new facets in it. There is a sense in which you can and should do this throughout the day—which is why the psalmist says "he meditates day and night" (Psalm 1:2)—but including meditation in that focused time with God can help focus it deeper on what God is saying to you through scripture.

At the other end of the scale there is what could be called "macrostudy". You should understand that the authors of the Bible didn't really write verses. They wrote letters and books and poems and messages to people. While microstudy is very valuable, you should always recognize that the writers of the Bible were conveying a message through the totality of the books they wrote more than through the individual sentences. Study of those sentences is valuable because we better grasp what they were saying in detail, but we must not miss the forest for the trees. We must also study books.

One of the best approaches to macrostudy is to read a single book of the Bible straight through, quickly, repeatedly. As you read it through, you will start to hear the message of the book as a whole. As you go back to the beginning and read it again, you will see things you missed the first time through. You will realize that things that were stated strongly at the end were foreshadowed at the beginning, or things driven home in the early pages were echoed later. You will see themes running through the book as in Philippians where Paul constantly comes back to reminding them to rejoice. From this you will begin to understand why the author wrote the book, what he was trying to say through it, and how the book as a whole applies to you.

Some of the larger books don't lend themselves to reading through in a single sitting. Still, macrostudy is important here as well. Determine to read for so long, or so many chapters, or so many pages, each day, and go through the book several times at that rate. Even though the reading is interrupted, taking it in large chunks and repeating it several times will bring out information you missed on a single reading.

There is a place in all this for reference books. A good commentary can give you much that is useful. Understanding who were the first readers of a book and what was happening where they lived can open the meanings of difficult passages— such as understanding that a Corinthian Christian woman would be disgraced by a shaved head because that was the mark of a pagan temple prostitute. There may be nuances in the ancient languages which your translation cannot adequately capture; sometimes there are things to learn from examining variations in the original text. For example, the number 666 in Revelation appears in some manuscripts as 616; the best explanation for this is that both numbers represent the name of Caesar Nero, depending on whether it is the subject or the object of the sentence. These things you can learn from books about the

Bible, such as commentaries, introductions, atlases, and Bible dictionaries. Never let the reference book replace the Bible, and never take the reference book as Bible; always examine the text yourself, and come to your own conclusions about it. References have their place; they need to have their place, but they must be kept in their place.

All of this may seem overwhelming. I have tried to give you approaches which will serve you for years to come. It may be that today you will start with something smaller and more manageable. The value of reading a little bit each day cannot be discounted or underestimated. A chapter a day is a good measure; time can also work, such as determining that fifteen or twenty minutes will be spent reading (and the remaining time in prayer and worship).

There is no part of the Bible which has no value to us; however, there are parts that are easier to understand, which contain more value to us specifically (other parts may have had more value to God's people before us). The epistles, and particularly those of Paul, were written specifically to Christians; as such, you will find that they address issues in your life in a very focused and rich way. The gospels present the person of Jesus, the very image of God in the flesh, most clearly, and so are also easier to grasp. However, at different times in your life you may find the heart of God in the prophets, the joy of salvation in the psalms and poetic books, the wisdom of God in Proverbs. The histories of Israel and the books of the Law contain some parts which are less inspiring, but also contain great truths which show aspects of God we might otherwise miss. These Old Testament scriptures were the Bible for the first Christians who wrote the New Testament, and in these pages they saw the gospel we preach. At different times in your life different parts of the Bible will open themselves to you.

You should not despair of reading if it seems dry, just as you should not despair of prayer or worship if you don't feel the presence of God. We do not read and pray and worship because we feel the benefit, but because we know the benefit is real whether we feel it or not. It may be that as you read you will see new vistas opening before your mind, aspects of truth you have not considered before, or new depths to concepts you already grasp. It may instead be that the words of your reading will come back to you later in the day, or the week, showing you how what you have seen in scripture touches your life. It may even be that you will never consciously be aware of the impact some passages have had on you. That impact is still there. God has promised that "it is God who is at work in you, both to will and to work for His good pleasure." (Philippians 2:13) We cannot help but see Him when we come to Him; we cannot help but be changed when we see Him. At times it will seem as if there is nothing, no presence of God, no new insight, no deeper understanding. However, "we walk by faith, not by sight." (II Corinthians 5:7) "Faith is the assurance of things hoped for, the conviction of things not seen." (Hebrews 11:1) That is, faith is a way of knowing things we didn't see for ourselves. Faith is relying on what we have been told, knowing that what God tells us must be true. Thus since God says that we will come to know Him through these things, we know that whether we have the sense of coming to know Him better or not, we are coming to know Him better when we read and study, pray and worship, memorize and meditate.

At the same time, you should be mindful that the methods which have brought you to this point might not be adequate to carry you forward from here. Reading a chapter each day can be very helpful sometimes (and is certainly always better than not reading at all). Even learning the Bible verse that appears on your daily calendar can make a tremendous difference in your life. At some point, though, you will need to change the tools, move to other parts of the Bible, take a new approach. I have used all of the tools mentioned at some point in my life, and benefited greatly from each. I have not used them all at once, and there have been times in my life where each of them has let me down and I found I had to shift to another. You should find an approach to Bible study which works for you now, and you should use that approach while it works, but you should expect that at some point you will abandon this approach for another, not because the other approach is better or the old approach is insufficient, but because to see more of God you need new ways of looking.

There are many translations from which you can read, and Christians will argue about which is best. There is no best translation. For microstudy, it is better to have what is called a "modern committee translation" which attempts to render the text as close to a word-for-word basis as the differences in language will allow. The New American Standard Bible has been praised for this, but the New International Version, the Revised Standard Version, and others are very good. These translations have the disadvantage that they are often difficult to read, and do not always convey ideas easily and quickly enough for understanding in quick reading. On the other side, "paraphrases" and other looser translations which attempt to bring scripture across idea for idea can be quite good for macrostudy, as reading these is generally easier and so flows quickly through the key thoughts of the author. The Living Bible and the Message were made for this kind of reading, and many other translations have leaned more toward readability than precision in rendering the text. These are not good choices for memorization or microstudy, and there is a tendency in reading these that you will see what the translator thought the words meant more strongly than what you might have thought they meant were you able to look at the original words yourself. Still, you will absorb the overarching ideas of each book more readily from these translations, and they have their place.

It is helpful in the long term to do all your memorization from the same translation. You will always know what translation it is you are quoting, and in years to come when you are trying to recall where a verse you remember is found you will know which concordance will most likely find it by the words you remember. Because memorization is best for microstudy, translations which are better for such close scrutiny are better choices for memorization.

I would discourage most modern readers from using the King James or Authorized Version. Understand that at the time it was translated it was the best English translation available. However, there are problems with it. One problem that is not easy to solve springs from the fact that they did not have our tools for textual criticism. Scholars today spend many hours pouring over hundreds of ancient copies in the original languages and of translations made in the first centuries of the church, trying to reconstruct the original text in those places in which a word or phrase is uncertain, or what may once have been someone's note scribbled in a margin has become part of the text, or a copyist misread something. Although these are not usually major differences, if you are studying the words in detail you want to be as certain as possible that you are looking at the original words, and the King James scholars had only a few copies, and did not know which were the older and better when they made their decisions. Several other otherwise excellent older translations, such as the Revised Version, the original American Standard Version, and Young's Literal Translation, also suffer this problem, although to a lesser degree.

Even, though, were we to conclude that none of these minor differences will matter, we must recognize that the King James translation is now over four hundred years old. Certainly it has stood the test of time for its beauty and usefulness; but language itself has changed in many ways, and words which were used one way then are used quite another way now. One example will make this clear; but there are hundreds of places where nuances in the way we use words today are different from the way they used them, which may lead to wrong understandings of the text.

Many preachers, raised on the King James Bible, will quote that we should "Abstain from all appearance of evil." (I

Thessalonians 5:22, KJV) From this they will explain that as Christians we should not do anything that even looks bad, that someone might interpret as wrong or sinful; they will then build from this arguments against being involved in many things which they personally don't like and would like to label "unchristian" but for which they have no clearer biblical argument. There is certainly a place for taking care how our actions appear to others, which will be examined later in this book. However, this verse does not mean that at all. The natural reading of that rendering of the sentence, in our way of reading the language, might be paraphrased, "Avoid anything that even looks evil;" however, the meaning which the translators intended to convey, the meaning of the Greek text and the way it is stated in every other translation, would be correctly understood as "Avoid anything that is evil, no matter what it looks like." It is not things that appear evil, but evil no matter how it appears, against which this verse warns. Few of us would dare attempt to understand Shakespeare without notes which explain what he meant by particular words and phrases, yet too many of us assume that the King James translators used words exactly as they would be used today.

Regarding other books, it is obvious that I believe in the value of Christian books. You are reading evidence of that right now. I have read hundreds of books by many authors which have helped my understanding of scripture and of our faith, and some I have read repeatedly over the years and found them valuable each time. Such books should never replace scripture, though. They should only supplement it. Even so called "devotional" books, which can be very valuable in many ways, should not be considered a substitute for personal reading of the Bible. The Bible is the picture of God, the book in which He reveals Himself to us. Other books are at best second-hand accounts, descriptions of God by others who have seen Him, and suffer from reliability. The writers may have seen something in God that they needed to see for their ministry, their place in the body of Christ, which is not what God would show you; they may have misunderstood what they saw, or

31

failed to see the whole picture. That doesn't make their insights useless; they are very useful, as part of an effort to know God better. They need to be balanced by other writers who saw different aspects, and even more by the truth itself. You need to look intently at the Word of God and see Him in it for yourself. Knowing what others have seen is helpful, but does not replace this personal time with God.

Profitable, Edifying, and Necessary

"All things are lawful...."

Paul writes these words not fewer than four times in First Corinthians, and he means them. We have already explained that the Christian life is not about keeping rules, but about loving each other. Paul is telling us that there is nothing we are "not allowed" to do. Nothing is forbidden.

Yet each time he says it, he qualifies it. Those qualifications are a vital facet of our understanding of how we conduct our lives.

"All things are lawful for me, but not all things are profitable." (I Corinthians 6:12) "All things are lawful, but not all things are profitable." (I Corinthians 10:23) Paul twice states that some things are not profitable; he says it in such a way as to suggest that we should prefer to do things which are profitable over things which are not.

Something is profitable if it benefits the one involved. That is, if an action I take does something good for me, I profited from it, and it is therefore profitable. It is better to do things that benefit you in some way than to do things that do not benefit you. These are profitable things.

We still need to understand what this means, however. It is easy to imagine that something is profitable because it pays us in some way; but profit isn't a matter of income but of net, that is, the balance of what is gained against what is lost. Paul will say later in this same letter, "if I give all my possessions to feed the poor, and if I surrender my body to be burned, but do not have love, it profits me nothing." (I Corinthians 13:3) Jesus asked, "what does it profit a man to gain the whole world, and forfeit his soul?" (Mark 8:36) Profit is not measured by what you get from what you do, but by what you get against what it cost. If you lost more than you gained, there was no profit in it.

Something is profitable only if in the long term the benefit exceeds the cost.

It is also wise to consider what in accounting terms are called "opportunity costs". This is an important investment concept. In financial terms, it means that if you used your money in a manner which earned you some money, but you could have used it in a different manner which would have earned you more money, you lost money—you lost the money you could have made had you done the other thing.

In our lives, we also have opportunity costs. It is not easy to know always what is the best use of our time or our money. Many people complain that they wasted their lives working toward riches they will never enjoy because they lost their families through neglect or accident; yet money is necessary, and it is difficult to know when you have enough to meet your needs in this life. It is important to spend time on spiritual things, prayer and study, fellowship and ministry, but there are earthly matters that need attention as well. Life is serious, and there are many things that demand our attention, but people need time to relax, and recreation, hobbies, and leisure activities are a necessary part of physical and mental health. In short, there are many ways in which we profit, and we cannot neglect one entirely, but we must consider whether time spent in one activity might be more profitably spent in another.

Thus the question, "Is this profitable?" is important in understanding what we should do.

"All things are lawful, but not all things edify." (I Corinthians 10:23) To edify is to build. The building that we are building is the Church of Christ. That is, when Paul speaks of edifying, he usually means that we are to do those things which cause the Church to grow and become stronger and more unified—in short, things by which we help each other.

Immediately upon saying that not all things edify, he says, "Let no one seek his own good, but that of his neighbor." (I Corinthians 10:24) He speaks often of this aspect of building the body of Christ. He will later write to them that God gave him "authority...for building you up" (II Corinthians 10:8, 13:10), and that he had been "speaking in Christ; and all for your upbuilding." (II Corinthians 12:19) When he speaks to the Ephesians about ministries he gives their purpose as "the equipping of the saints for the work of service, to the building up of the body of Christ." (Ephesians 4:12) That concept of building the body of Christ is one of the key measures of what we do. Does this draw the Church together and make it stronger, or does it drive us apart and cause pain and division?

Remember, the Church is built like a building, but also like a body. Each of us is part of the whole, but each serves a different function. A modern building would not be much use without plumbing, wiring, framing, flooring, walls—yet not one of those parts of the building would be much use without the rest. In Paul's analogy, we are like a body, and we need the feet and hands as much as the eyes and ears.

In other words, we need each other, not merely because we need people, but because we need people whose strengths are different from ours, and for whom we can provide the strengths for their weaknesses. The Body of Christ is a collection of people who fit together in unexpected ways, each giving to all, all giving to each. Actions which are edifying contribute to that unity of the faith, drawing us together and making others whole.

As mentioned, edification is the purpose of ministry. That is, pastors, teachers, evangelists, whatever ministries are found within the church, are there to build up the body. That is accomplished largely by building up the members of the body, individually as well as collectively. Actions may be edifying if they help a single person, or if they benefit millions. They edify by helping any one person move closer to his place within the body, or by drawing together all into a closer relationship with each other. Speaking of church meetings, Paul says, "Let all things be done for edification." (I Corinthians 14:26) Everything we do is tested by whether it builds the church.

Note that Paul says his authority is "for building up and not for tearing down." (II Corinthians 13:10) This is the other side of edifying: not only do we prefer actions which would build up, but we need to avoid actions which would tear down.

Paul also warns us to be careful how we build. There is only one foundation, of course, whether for the Church as a whole or for individuals within it. "Now if any man builds on the foundation with gold, silver, precious stones, wood, hay, straw, each man's work will become evident; for the day will show it because it is to be revealed with fire, and the fire itself will test the quality of each man's work. If any man's work which he has built on it remains, he will receive a reward. If any man's work is burned up, he will suffer loss; but he himself will be saved, yet so as through fire." (I Corinthians 3:10-15) Our actions, our choices, can make us better by building within others those eternal treasures. The good things we build will be eternal; the things we build that are worthless will be lost.

How do we build? "Knowledge makes arrogant, but love edifies." (I Corinthians 8:1) There may be something of a pun here; it might be translated "Knowledge puffs up, but love builds up" (see I Corinthians 8:1, KJV). We build up the body of Christ by love, expressing that love as we should.

Many Christians are asking entirely the wrong kinds of questions. Are Christians permitted to drink wine, or coffee, or beer? Does God forbid smoking cigarettes? How far can you go on a first date, or with your fiancé, if you are a Christian? What clothing does God permit? These questions fundamentally misunderstand the heart of the gospel. Law is about limits and license, about going so far and no further. These questions are like asking how close you can get to the edge of the cliff without being in danger of falling, how hard you can push against God before you push yourself out of His hand. The gospel does not lead us to ask how far we can run away from God before we are out of His reach. It invites us to discover how close we can get to God and to each other. Too many of us are asking whether we can get away with choices God might disapprove. We should be asking what choices will bring us closer to Him, what actions will build our faith, what conduct will encourage and strengthen those around us and bring us all into greater unity in the faith. Christianity is not about how far we can pursue our own selfish desires while staying within the bounds of God's expectations. It is about how near we can draw to God when that becomes the object of everything we do.

There is one more caveat Paul presents. "All things are lawful, but I will not be mastered by anything." (I Corinthians 6:12) There is nothing in life that Christians cannot do. However, there must be nothing in life that we cannot not do. It is for freedom that we have been set free. God did not do all of this for us so that we could be slaves, but that we could be set free. If anything is compelling or irresistible, it fails this test.

It is easy to think that we know the kinds of things that enslave people. Clearly there are physical addictions, from cigarettes and alcohol to street drugs. There are sexual compulsions, whether clearly aberrant or socially acceptable. There are psychological compulsions such as compulsive gambling. In creating these lists of the obvious, however, we are often trying to convince ourselves that this does not apply to us. It applies to everyone. Whether you are a slave to fashion or a compulsive slob, a spendthrift or a miser, everything in your life should pass this test: am I the master, or am I the servant? Do I do this by choice, am I able to choose not to do this, or does this drive and control me?

It is these things which we most commonly find God asking us to surrender. It might be a hobby; it might be a relationship; it might be a habit, or a preferred form of entertainment. It might even be a favorite treat. In every Christian life God will at some point step in and insist that we stop doing something which is not wrong (remember, all things are lawful) but which fails this test. We discover that we are not able to be free of it; we learn that we really don't want to be free of it, that we enjoy our slavery or fear the loss of security it provides. It is here that we fight our toughest battles, for they are battles which we would choose to lose but that we know God is expecting us to win. We embrace slavery for a host of reasons, but God commands us to be free. So we face this test, and in each place in our lives we ask ourselves whether this is more important to us than God, whether this is something we could be without, whether this is something we are free to choose and to choose not, or something that chooses for us.

Nothing in your life should ever be more important than God. If you are a slave to your job, God may ask you to quit. If you are a slave to your friends, God may require that you stop seeing them. Whatever enslaves you, God wants you free, and although all things are lawful, if there is anything you cannot imagine not doing, it is probably that which is your master, and that from which you must be freed.

We have seen three tests by which we can measure our conduct: is it profitable, is it edifying, and does it master us? We should be doing things which are profitable and edifying and avoiding things that master us. Does this completely define the boundaries of what Christians should and should not do?

For better or worse, Christian life is not so simple. We cannot replace one law with another, for law is still law. In defending his ministry, Paul says, "Boasting is necessary, though it is not profitable." (II Corinthians 12:1) He tells the Philippians that although it would be better for him to die and be with the Lord, "yet to remain on in the flesh is more necessary for your sake." (Philippians 1:24) There are things we must do which would not be our first choice, things which

38

don't benefit us and don't help the church, but which must be done. I imagine that paying bills is probably in this category (although my wife argues that paying bills is profitable); for some, earning a living is a hardship that gives little return for the trouble. Paul never clearly says what things might be necessary, but just the suggestion that there are these things should make us aware that Christian conduct is never so simple as a few rules that govern everything. What is profitable, what is edifying, what masters us—these are tools which point us in the right direction, which are right nearly every time. However, our walk in God requires much of us, that we read and pray, that we think, that we listen. Doing what is profitable and edifying and avoiding what enslaves us are valuable principles which will answer many of the questions you face; but walking in the Spirit is more than applying principles.

Weaker Brothers

In our Christian walk we are always to have respect for the weaker brother. Some say that this means we must never do anything that might cause someone else to stumble, even if it is a good thing for us to do. Others observe that such a rule would prevent us from doing anything whatsoever. What is this weaker brother idea about?

It comes in large part from a very long section of First Corinthians, in which Paul addresses the very specific problem of eating meat that has been sacrificed to a pagan god, and the general reality of the freedom in Christ. The two issues are inseparable, and it is important to see them together.

Corinth was one of the strongholds of pagan religion in Paul's day. Much of what Paul writes to the Corinthians is about how they can be Christian in the midst of a pagan world. This problem arose, and it appears that the church decided to send a letter to Paul asking how to handle it, along with a few other matters. Pagans, much as the Jews, would make sacrifices to their gods. Bulls and cows and chickens and sheep and many other perfectly healthy animals were slaughtered to petition, appease, or thank the gods, and the carcasses left with the priests. Some of these were burned on the altars, and some became food for the priests, but there was a lot of meat in these sacrifices. For many good reasons, the temples would pass the meat on to butcher shops in the area, often at a low price, where anyone could buy good meat cheaply. It wasn't always labeled, but everyone in Corinth knew the way it worked.

Eating the meat of a sacrifice was a way in which priests and worshippers of certain religions participated in the ceremonies. Thus in the minds of many pagans, it was an extra blessing to eat such meat. If this were so, though, it would mean that anyone who ate such meat was participating in the sacrifice and thus in the religious rituals of the pagan temple. Or would it? Some in Corinth argued that it was all nonsense, that the gods of the pagans were nothing and didn't matter, and that it was good sense to buy meat when it was on special, particularly if you knew it had been from an animal that had been inspected by a priest and determined to be healthy just before it was butchered. Others insisted that to eat such meat was to invite damnation, to be involved in communion with false gods, to be unfaithful to Christ. Paul was asked to settle this question.

The answer Paul gives has been applied to everything and anything about which Christians have been uncertain. If it has anything about it that is questionable, the specter is raised that it might lead someone astray, and so should be avoided. Yet it is clear that there are things we do, things we must do, which have the potential to lead others into sin. Should married people refrain from showing affection in public because single people might be tempted toward fornication? Someone has satirically suggested that children are a reminder of sex, and should be kept secreted away somewhere so as not to cause such temptations. This may seem silly, but just about anything you can do or even think can be a temptation for someone. I once counseled a man with a foot fetish, who derived sexual pleasure from people removing their shoes. Does this mean that none of us should ever remove our shoes again to protect this one person? Applying this idea seems to lead to all sorts of confusion.

Yet the teaching about the weaker brother is important in our lives, and does apply to all things, if we understand it aright.

The question first appears in the eighth chapter of First Corinthians. As it spans three chapters, you should review it in its entirety. The key points are sometimes missed, so we will focus on those.

When Paul says that "we all have knowledge," (I Corinthians 8:1), he is agreeing with one side of the argument: as Christians, we all know that we are free, and that we can act from freedom instead of slavery. Knowledge is not everything, though; Paul commends love above knowledge.

He then expresses the view that idols are nothing, and thus anything sacrificed to an idol is no different from anything slaughtered in any other fashion. He agrees that even if such gods exist, they have no power over us, and we should feel free to eat anything sacrificed to them because they can't touch us.

It's not so cut and dried as that, though. "However, not all men have this knowledge; but some, being accustomed to the idol until now, eat food as if it were sacrificed to an idol; and their conscience being weak is defiled." (I Corinthians 8:7) Note that this is clearly speaking of Christians (because it says they thought of idols as real "until now", emphasized in 8:11), and not of the people in the world; yet it says that we don't all have the knowledge which a moment ago he said we did have. If we all have knowledge, how is it that some do not have this knowledge?

The answer lies in the fact that we are individuals, each with his own individual history. Some of us can be told, and told again, and told a hundred times, that idols can't hurt us, but if we have spent years of our lives believing and trusting idols it is difficult to repent of such beliefs overnight. Certainly we do believe that the idol is nothing; we don't believe it so utterly that they don't affect us. Because we have this long history of trusting idols, we have a weak spot, a place at which we are easily tempted, specifically in connection with trusting idols.

"But food will not commend us to God; we are neither the worse if we do eat, nor the better if we do not eat." (I Corinthians 8:8) There are two levels to these words which must be understood if we are to grasp the concept of the weaker brother fully.

Paul is saying, on one level, that it doesn't matter whether or not we eat, in the sense that we can and should feel free to eat

42

such meat sacrificed to idols because it can't hurt us. Note that well: eating meat sacrificed to idols cannot hurt us in any way in and of itself. The meat is safe; the idols are nothing. Those stronger brothers who go ahead and eat are right. They are free to eat.

The other level is equally important, however: we are free to decide not to eat it. Some of the stronger brothers in this matter were eagerly encouraging others to eat the meat with them. The argument is this: if you are fully mature and fully trusting in Christ, you know that this meat can't hurt you; therefore, it is an important expression of your freedom from the slavery of idolatry that you eat this meat, so that you show God how free you are. Paul is saying that just as there is nothing wrong with intentionally eating meat you know was offered to idols, there is equally nothing wrong with choosing not to eat such meat, and eating it does nothing to strengthen your relationship with God. If you think it might be a problem for you, personally, to eat such meat, then don't eat it. God doesn't expect you to flaunt your freedom to prove you believe in it. You can eat or not eat; it's all the same in spiritual terms. No one can tell you that you are less spiritual because you choose not to eat meat offered to idols, or that you are more spiritual because you choose to do so.

I wish to step away from Corinth for a moment and put some modern concerns to this. Over the years many preachers have thought that one thing or another seemed in their judgment to have some connection to the devil. Having made this determination (on whatever basis) they then insisted that because there was this potential connection to Satanism, no matter how tenuous, Christians should have nothing to do with this thing. These things have been as diverse as movie theaters (regardless of the film playing), rock and roll music (even if proclaiming Christ), role playing games (of any kind), fantasy and science fiction literature (even by noted Christian writers)— and the list grows.

We could write volumes arguing the merits of each case, whether rock and roll or role playing games or anything else mentioned is Satanic. The fact is that everything in this world is tainted by the world, the flesh, and the devil—even our churches and Bible studies and ministries. Some things that contain much that has the potential for evil also have great potential for good. In the end, however, none of the things for which this argument is raised even approaches the level of participating in pagan rituals by eating the sacrifices from the altars. Paul has an open and shut case here: this is a knowing and intentional participation in pagan ritual, done by Christians whose defense is that while they might be present for the ritual and participating in it, they know full well that God is above all this. They claim they can go into the temples of the idols themselves, sit at the tables, and eat the food, without in any way dishonoring God or threatening their salvation. There is nothing wrong with what they are doing. Shockingly, Paul agrees with them. It is perfectly acceptable for them to do this, because they are safe in God's hands and the false gods cannot have them, cannot touch them, as long as they are doing all things with thankfulness to the true God.

If it's true for meat offered to idols, then it is clearly true for any of those things which we think might have some sort of pagan or satanic connection. We are free to enjoy them, to share in them, as long as we ourselves understand that God is God, as long as we are not participating in the attitude of worship of false gods but only enjoying the free food or the entertainment or whatever the benefit may be.

However, the weaker brother argument doesn't end here. It's only beginning.

"But take care that this liberty of yours does not somehow become a stumbling block to the weak." (I Corinthians 8:9) With these words, Paul presents the caveat. You might be free to sit in that temple and enjoy the free food, but if I use to be a devout pagan worshipper and I see you there, this becomes a problem for me. It could be that I would be encouraged to join you there, at that table—but although in your mind that which you are eating is just free food, in my mind it is a sacrifice to a god, participation in the worship of the idol. So while you partake with thanksgiving toward God and enjoyment of the meal, I am caught in the feelings of my old beliefs, in reverence and awe for some deity I have tried to put behind me. Your freedom is becoming a snare which will trap me in my old beliefs. "Therefore, if food causes my brother to stumble, I will never eat meat again, so that I will not cause my brother to stumble." (I Corinthians 8:13)

It is, however, clear that Paul does eat meat. He doesn't sit in pagan temples and help himself to what is served there, perhaps, but he does preach in and around those temples, and he does eat meat some of which might well have come from such butchers. Paul is immersed in pagan society, becoming "all things to all men, that I may by all means save some." (I Corinthians 9:22) If meat causes someone to stumble, why does Paul eat meat? The answer is simple: whether or not Paul eats meat, and whether or not you or I eat meat offered to idols, or listen to rock music, or watch movies or read books or play games is not the issue. The issue is whether we encourage the weaker brother to do so. If those who are weak toward this feel pressured to do it, it destroys them.

Paul suddenly launches into a discussion of his apostleship; many who read First Corinthians think that he's changed the subject, that he is now defending his apostleship against charges that he is not really an apostle. He has not changed the subject. He is using himself as an example. In chapter nine he will make several important points which stem from his assertion that he is an apostle, no less an apostle than any other. Being an apostle means having certain rights, such as the right to be paid by those to whom you are preaching, to be supported through the ministry, and to support your family from it. However, Paul has refused to allow the Corinthian church to support his ministry up to now, and has no intention of changing that presently. He has the right to impose on them, but chooses not to do so. He makes that choice because he does not wish outsiders to see him as someone who is preaching for the money. There are other churches that support him, and he works to support himself, but although he has every right to ask Corinth to pay him for his labors there, he does not do so because he does not want that to be an issue.

This is not his practice everywhere, however. It is his practice in Corinth. The Macedonian churches are supporting him; he receives support from his home church in Antioch; he is about to write a letter to Rome asking that they would support his efforts to preach to them and beyond them to Spain. It was Paul's perception that money would be a stumbling block to some of those in Corinth, and so he was careful to prevent it from being an issue there.

Note that the money issue is in no way suspect. It doesn't smack of Satanism or paganism or anything else. Paul is expanding his "weaker brother" and "stumbling blocks" argument beyond things that have some hint of evil to touch things that are good, even things, as he emphasizes, commanded by God. "The Lord directed those who proclaim the gospel to get their living from the gospel." (I Corinthians 9:14) In a sense, Paul is going against the commandment of God in order to avoid creating a stumbling block for those in Corinth.

He has more to say before he returns to the pagan altars; he lists things which we should avoid, things which might enslave us, things which would pull us down. He speaks of disciplining himself, running the race and winning the prize. He warns us against idolatry and immorality, but also against grumbling and trying God's patience. "Now these things happened to them as an example," he tells us, "and they were written for our instruction." (I Corinthians 10:11) It is not that these are laws we are to follow, but, as we said before, they are pictures of what God wants from His people, what God is like, and what it is like to live in love or without love. If we are tempted toward these things, we want to move away from those things which so entice us.

Paul eventually comes back to those pagan altars, and notes that they are sacrifices to demons. "I do not want you to be sharers in demons." (I Corinthians 10:20) Paul is saying that those free meals at the temples do have a Satanic connection, and it would be better to avoid them. However, he also says, "Eat anything that is sold in the meat market without asking questions for conscience' sake" (I Corinthians 10:25), and goes on to suggest that you should freely eat meat served by anyone with whom you happen to be dining. The demon is nothing, and the eating of the sacrifice is nothing. It is only the visible participation in the worship in the temple Paul says to avoid. Don't practice idolatry, and don't be seen to practice idolatry, but don't worry about any ill that might come from participation in such practices that is removed as far as that. Note that this is still "participation" in the mind of those who believe. "But if anyone says to you, 'This is meat sacrificed to idols,' do not eat it, for the sake of the one who informed you" (I Corinthians 10:28)—that is, if you know there's someone here who can't reconcile the freedom of Christ with those things they practiced in their old lives, have respect for that weakness and don't offend them. "I mean not your conscience, but the other man's; for why is my freedom judged by another's conscience? If I partake with thankfulness, why am I slandered concerning that for which I give thanks? Whether, then, you eat or drink or whatever you do, do all to the glory of God." Paul is telling us that we should feel free to do whatever God has allowed us to do, and not worry about what someone else might think, but only to do so in times, places, and ways that aren't going to offend people who really cannot handle them.

In all this he is telling us that it is the weaker brother who chooses not to do these things. It is not that the one who does not eat meat or listen to rock music or play certain kinds of games has reached a higher level of spiritual maturity measured by greater strength; if they have reached a higher level of

47

spiritual maturity here, it is in that they have recognized in themselves a weakness, an inability to stand against temptation in a particular area of their lives, and so have chosen to avoid those temptations. That is the maturity of recognizing your own weaknesses, not of finding a greater strength.

In the midst of this, Paul says, "Therefore let him who thinks he stands take heed that he does not fall." (I Corinthians 10:12) In saying this, he warns us of a side of the weaker brother of which we must be aware: we do not know whether we are the weaker or the stronger brother; we do not know what will tempt us or cause us to fall. Freedom is to be enjoyed, but not with such reckless abandon that we leave ourselves vulnerable to sin. In his next words, "No temptation has taken you but such as is common to man," (I Corinthians 10:13) he makes it clear that we are all alike, we all face the same kinds of things. That means that although you may be the stronger brother in one thing, there is something in life where you are the weaker brother, some temptation which will destroy you which would not even touch me. That doesn't mean I can't do what would destroy you, or that you can't do what would destroy me; it means that each of us must understand that there are things others can do that we cannot, and things we can do that others cannot. "God is faithful, who will not allow you to be tempted beyond what you are able, but with the temptation will provide the way of escape also, so that you will be able to endure it. (I Corinthians 10:13) When the temptation comes, you must recognize it and flee from it; when you see your weakness, you must protect yourself in that area and stay away from things that would tempt you. God will make it possible for you to stand for as long as you must stand, and to run when you can stand no longer—it is not inevitable that you will fall when confronted by your weakness. However, you must not think yourself invincible.

It is here that our rules and regulations, our codes of conduct, find some validity. I may have discovered that due to my personal weakness, it is best for me never to listen to secular music, or watch movies with occultic themes, or dine in a restaurant where liquor is served, or participate in coed athletic activities. These things may become rules in my personal code of conduct by which I protect myself from temptation: by not crossing this line, I am confident that I will never reach that one. You may learn from my rules. By seeing how I conduct myself you have an example of how one Christian attempts to maintain a holy life, and you may find something worthy of imitation. However, neither you nor I must ever confuse my rules with some sort of new Christian Law. These are not more than those things which God has required of me, and possibly much less than that, ways in which I have limited myself to protect myself from that which might cause me to stumble. Neither of us must ever think that God judges us by my rules—or by yours, or anyone else's. Such rules are a weak human way to protect ourselves against human weakness. They are not therefore unimportant or useless, but we must not think them more than they are.

Paul revisits this matter of the weaker brother when he writes to Rome. There he says, "The one who eats is not to regard with contempt the one who does not eat, and the one who does not eat is not to judge the one who eats, for God has accepted him. Who are you to judge the servant of another? To his own master he stands or falls; and he will stand, for the Lord is able to make him stand." (Romans 14:3-4) In Romans, Paul applies this to clean and unclean foods, vegetarianism, the observance of Sabbaths and holidays, and he suggests that it extends to all things.

He tells us that the strong and the weak have obligations to each other. Those of us who are strong, who can do what others cannot, may not look down on those who cannot do what we can do. At the same time, we who are weak cannot condemn those who do what we cannot. It is not our job to decide what others can do. It is our job to live godly lives as God has directed us, individually, and not to impose that which he

49

requires of us or that which we have learned will protect us on the actions of others.

He tells us that each of us is answerable to God, but not to each other, that it is wrong for any of us to presume to tell another what to do, what God requires, in some legalistic sense. God deals with us individually, and brings us together into unity based on our individual strengths and weaknesses. He does not give us uniform codes of conduct that we all must follow, but an understanding that to love Him and to love each other is the foundation of all we do, and the freedom to do whatever expresses that love, whatever builds us up as individuals and as a body, whatever expresses the new creation within us.

He tells us that the strong and the weak are both accepted by God as they are. The weak do not need to become strong, nor the strong weak. Those who are tempted by some things do not have to force themselves to face those situations to be strengthened, and those who are not tempted by those same things do not need to stay away from them in deference to those who are weak. We need to respect and love each other; we need to recognize that some have freedom in one area and some in another, and all have weakness in one area or another, and all are strong in one way or another.

It is in some ways a balancing act. "For if because of food your brother is hurt, you are no longer walking according to love" (Romans 14:15)—a clear call to act in a way that will not bring temptation to your weaker brother. Yet immediately he says, "Therefore, do not let what is for you a good thing be spoken of as evil." (Romans 14:16) The freedom God gives us is for us to enjoy, and not for others to take from us. "So then we pursue the things which make for peace and the building up of one another." (Romans 14:19) It is not primarily about deciding what to do; it is about learning to build each other up, about doing things that draw us together and strengthen the body. If we do this, then we can understand how some can

50

enjoy the freedoms others cannot without one causing the other to stumble.

Humility

We have mentioned that on one occasion Paul said boasting was necessary, although humility has long been known as one of the Christian virtues. This concept is greatly misunderstood, and leads many to foolish statements and misplaced judgments. While in some ways it may not immediately seem related to Christian conduct, it is related to that which is profitable and edifying, and to knowing who we are under God.

The first thing to understand about humility is that it is not seeing yourself as worthless or useless. That is not how God sees you, and it is not how He expects you to see yourself. To show this, we will take a look at a big story in a small book.

The story is about a slave whose name was Useful. This name turned out to be rather ironic, because he proved to be rather useless as a slave. He ran away from his master, and hid in one of the big cities.

Perhaps he was arrested; perhaps he had met the preacher before; or perhaps it was just one of those unexplained and unexpected events. However it came about, Useful ran into Paul, who was in prison at the time. Then having encountered Paul, he heard the gospel and became a Christian.

As it happened, Paul knew Useful's owner, a man whose name was very like Friend. Friend had in fact become a Christian through Paul's ministry some years before. Useful was now also a Christian, and it was obvious that he was going to have to go back to Friend to face whatever consequences would come from his actions.

Useful certainly had reason to be frightened. Slaves were absolute property of their masters in those days, and although there were many runaways living in the cities the Empire permitted slave owners great freedom in how such things were punished. Most runaway slaves, once recovered, were put to death rather painfully. For Friend to have beaten Useful very severely but spared his life would have been merciful by the standards of the age. Paul decided to write a letter to Friend and ask him to go beyond that, to embrace Useful as a lost brother instead of a runaway slave. That letter teaches us much about who we are and how we relate to each other. Useful, in Greek, is Onesimus, and the Friend of Paul is named Philemon.

As he often does in his letters, Paul prays for Philemon, and writes what he prays. As also is often the case in Paul's letters, what he petitions God for the reader is the key point in the letter. This makes sense if you stop and think about it. Paul first says, "I pray that you will understand this, that this would be a reality in your life"—and then he, a teacher in addition to being an apostle, takes the rest of the letter to teach the reader what that means and how to embrace it. For Philemon, he prays "that the fellowship of your faith may become effective through the knowledge of every good thing which is in you for Christ's sake." (Philemon 6) If we can understand what this means, we can understand what Paul is trying to say to Philemon in this book, and why God chose to save this personal letter to one individual for the rest of us to read.

To understand this verse, though, we are going to have to use some techniques of microstudy, looking at each word and how they fit together, to draw out the meaning.

Fellowship is a word we toss about without much thought to the meaning. Someone has defined it as "two fellows in one ship." That's a cute definition that tells us much, but it's also the sort of catch phrase that makes us think we understand a word when we haven't truly grasped it. Fellowship is about being comrades, being in a close-knit relationship with each other. It is about sharing our lives with each other, finding that unity that goes beyond friendship. It is, in short, about becoming part of the same entity. It is about oneness. So this is about a kind of unity, a unity of our faith.

The word faith has several meanings in Greek, just as it does in English. The core of its meaning is the power of believing, that which we see in the words, "Have faith". That meaning doesn't fit here, though. It can also mean the content of what we believe, as in "the faith delivered to the saints." We today speak of a statement of faith, by which we mean words which define what we believe. That meaning doesn't work in this context well, either. There is a third meaning found in scripture. Faith can mean people who share the same beliefs. In our time, we speak of the Methodist faith or the Catholic faith, and understand that to mean a group of people who share similar beliefs. Paul similarly speaks of Christians as "the household of faith." That meaning fits this verse perfectly. The subject of the verse, the fellowship of your faith, is the knitting together in unity of those who share a belief in Christ.

So what does Paul pray about this? He prays that it may become effective. The first thing I see here is that if Paul is praying for it to become effective, it must be possible for it to be ineffective. In fact, I suspect that it must very commonly be ineffective, or Paul wouldn't be praying that it would become effective. What does this mean, though, effective or ineffective? It means whether or not it's working. Are we being knit together in unity, or are we just spending time in the same building together? Effective faith fellowship means that what we are doing is edifying, building up the church, drawing us together. Ineffective faith fellowship means that it is not.

So we would pray with Paul that the fellowship of our faith may become effective, for we all yearn for that unity of the Spirit, that feeling that we belong to some larger group that loves us and cares for us, and that we contribute something to it, something that makes us people who have value.

If we stop there, however, we miss something important. Paul not only prays that our faith would become effective; he also prays for the means by which that will happen. It comes through the knowledge of every good thing which is in you. Again we may need to take this apart to understand it.

There are good things in you. God wants you to know that. We know that He wants you to know that, because He speaks of them here; not only does He through Paul mention that there are good things in you, He makes a point that that knowledge of them is important. Further, He doesn't just want you to say yes, there are good things in me, if God says so it must be true. He wants you to know what those good things are. That's why He speaks of the knowledge of every good thing. He wants you to know each thing that is in you that is good. It is because you know that there are good things in you, and you know what they are, that the fellowship of your faith becomes effective.

You may be wondering what that has to do with anything, but it has to do with everything.

You are reading a book I wrote. Hopefully it has at least some small measure of value to you, that is, it is teaching something to you that will profit you and through that edify the church. I wrote this book because I am a teacher and a writer, someone who has skill in grasping and communicating ideas through words. I have studied the scriptures for many years, and with prayerful consideration and careful intelligent thought have discovered much of the truths you are reading. I put pen to paper, fingers to keyboard, to give these things to you because I knew there was something good in me. I knew that I had the intelligence to understand these things; I knew that I could effectively communicate them to you. Realizing that there were these good things in me, I used what God had given me to try to help you.

If I believed that there was nothing good in me, this book would not have been written. I had to believe that I had some understanding that would be helpful to others, and that I could convey that understanding to them, or I would not have written it. Before I could be any use to God or to you, I had to see that I had value, that there was something I could do, something good in me that made it possible for me to do something good for you.

For Philemon, it was the ability to love and forgive on which Paul was calling. Philemon had within himself the ability to receive Onesimus back "no longer as a slave, but more than a slave, a beloved brother, especially to me, but how much more to you." (Philemon 16) That love for each other is one of the good things God wants us to find that He has put within us. For each of us there are many more, and as we find them we discover what we can be for others, how we can edify, how we can build up the church.

What then? If humility is not an attitude of worthlessness that says there is nothing of any value in any of us, what is it? For that we have to turn to Philippians. "Have this attitude in yourselves which also was in Christ Jesus, who, although He existed in the form of God, did not regard equality a thing to be grasped, but emptied Himself, taking the form of a bond-servant, and being made in the likeness of men. Being found in appearance as a man, he humbled Himself by becoming obedient to the point of death, even death on a cross." (Philippians 2:5-8)

At no point did Jesus ever say that He was no one of any consequence. Never did He even think that He was powerless or useless or had nothing good in Himself. He always knew that He was the Son of God, the most important and powerful man ever to step on the earth; that He could destroy it all with a word, call an army of angels to His side in an instant. He was great, and he understood His own greatness completely. You will never find a place where Jesus said He had nothing good in Himself.

Yet He is our example of humility.

Humility is not declaring yourself to be worthless. If it were true that you are worthless there would be nothing humble about admitting it; if it's not true (and God, as we saw in Philemon, says it is not true) then it's outright lying and calling God a liar.

Humility starts with understanding that you are a great and valuable person, someone with talents and abilities that make you special, precious, important. Until you understand that you matter, that you are somebody with much to offer, you don't have the ability to be humble. It is as Winston Churchill once described one of his political opponents, "a modest man with much to be modest about". Those who are worthless cannot be humble; they can only be honest about being worthless. It is only those who are great who are in any position to be humble. You are great. You are God's creation, and you are God's child, and He has put good things in you which He wants you to discover. You must come to understand that you are great, wonderful, precious; you must see yourself as someone who has much to offer. Without that, you cannot begin to understand what it is to be humble.

Then, like Jesus, you don't deny who you are; you don't lie about what you have to offer; you don't pretend that you are not all the wonderful things God made you to be. You declare that you are who God made you, that you have abilities God gave you, that you have learned and are learning how to use them, to be the person God intends for you to be. From this pinnacle of greatness, from this position of knowing how wonderful you are, what a great creature God has made to bear your name, from this height, you can be humble. Humility is not saying that you have nothing to offer. Humility is declaring that you have great things to offer, and then using them in the service of others.

The picture of humility Paul gives us in Philippians is that of the Son of God, the most valuable Person in the universe and the one Person most able to understand just how infinitely valuable He is, giving His life to save us. Jesus didn't say that He felt sorry for us but couldn't do anything about it. He told us that He was the ultimate power behind everything, and then used all of that, every bit of Who He is, to serve us.

In the same way, Christian humility starts with understanding that each of us is important, each is great, each has talents and abilities that make us valuable; it then becomes humility when we take that self-importance and use it in the service of others—when we can see that no one is more important than we are, and use our importance to make the lives of others better.

That is effective faith fellowship. That is the reason humility is part of our understanding of Christian conduct. We must discover who we are so that we know how we can serve each other. It is by our discovery of our own value that we become able to build up the church into the unity of the faith, as we imitate Christ in using the very things which make us great to make others greater.

Guidance

One of the most confounding problems in the life of the ordinary Christian is the question of divine guidance. If you are one of those who wrestles with the difficulty of knowing where God is leading you, don't be embarrassed: this is often one of the most confounding problems in the life of the extraordinary Christian as well. I certainly cannot say that I have discovered all of the secrets to knowing God's will for my own life, let alone for anyone else. However, I have seen a few things about divine guidance which have helped me in the past, and which I expect will help me again in the future. They may be of some help to you, so I offer them for your edification.

True Christian conduct goes beyond what we should do generally to what God wants us to do moment by moment. One of the great problems with legalism is that it gives us an excuse to disobey God. That is, it is simple to set up the rules, the things you must do to be pleasing to God, and then to keep them—but in so doing ignore what He really wants you to do. Some people make an issue of tithing, of very specifically giving ten percent of their money to God. Not everyone can afford to give a tenth of what they have; for some, it would be a sin to take food from the mouths of their own children to give to others. Certainly God does lay it on the hearts of some to give ten percent, and to be very careful that they do not fail to do so. For many, though, that tithe becomes the excuse they have to avoid giving money where it is needed. It is not generosity but greed which motivates them to tithe. By giving so much they refuse to give more. The law of the tithe becomes an excuse, a way of pretending to obey God while in fact disobeying Him in the matter of giving. God wants us to give, and He may ask that we give ten percent—or twenty or thirty or even ninety percent of all we receive. The important thing is not that you measure what you give, but that you give what He asks of you.

That means knowing what God wants you to do, not just generally, but moment by moment. Christian conduct cannot be fully discussed without talking about Christian guidance.

Christians often speak of doors being opened or closed; they also speak of obstacles which must be overcome. This is all quite biblical. Paul spoke in the same terms in his epistles. At the same time, many Christians speak of "feeling led" to do one thing or another, or even of "not feeling led"—an extremely subjective conception of guidance, but not contrary to scripture either. Paul said that he found an open door in Troas, but found no rest for his spirit there. God often led his servants to places or into circumstances for His own purposes. This, though, creates the difficulty. How can you tell if you are being led, or if you have feelings of your own about the matter? At the same time, how can you distinguish an obstacle from a closed door? Obviously, if God has closed a door, it would be folly to attempt to force it open. On the other hand, God never promised that the path would always be smooth and easy. We have been told to expect suffering, persecution, and hardship—these are an essential part of the growth process of God's children, as we learn to persevere and press on for the prize.

No one can give you a magic key which will always answer this for you. Part of growth is learning to hear the still small voice of God above the storms of life, to recognize what is of God and what is not. Still, there are a few tools which can focus you to the right questions. Once you have the right questions, you are on your way to finding the right answers.

We have already mentioned two distinct forms of guidance. The one form is subjective guidance, the guidance which is best described as the witness of the Holy Spirit with our spirit which tells us that we are on the right path, or that the path before us is wrong. The other form we should call objective guidance. This is the type of guidance which we divine from our circumstances, from the events which surround us and the life we've been given. As one of my fellow students once said, if I believed it possible that I might be called by God to be a Roman Catholic priest, one of the first things I would check is whether I was born a man. I am neither a woman nor a Roman Catholic, and cannot say that God is not calling women to be Roman Catholic priests (nor that He is), but if I were a woman I would consider that strong evidence that God did not intend the Catholic priesthood for my life, and would require extraordinary guidance to persuade me that He did. Similarly, if I had very little money and could barely feed my family, I would not be easily persuaded that God wished for me to pledge ten thousand dollars to support the ministry of another, however worthy or needful. Circumstance, objective reality, is very much a part of our decisions concerning that which God intends for us.

Once we understand this balance between objective and subjective guidance, we are much further along the road to understanding God's plan for our lives.

Subjective guidance—the internal leading of the Spirit—extends beyond mere feelings which we have individually. We have been made part of the larger body of Christ for many reasons; one of these is to confirm us in the path we take, to help us see more clearly what God intends for us. However, let us first take a look at objective guidance.

Every day we face choices. We choose big things and little things. It is a mistake to believe that our choices in the larger questions are more important than our choices in the smaller ones. On one occasion not long ago, I was home working when a friend stopped by, hoping for some company on a trip to a bookstore. This required a choice. A door had opened for me to do something else, but the door was still open for me to continue that which I was doing. After all, I was working, and my work was not unimportant. On the other hand, my friendship also certainly was important, especially as this particular friend was avowedly not Christian. I did not wish to leave what I was doing, and could easily have told him that I regrettably was very busy; nor did I wish to blow him off, or to discourage him from considering me in the future. I chose to go with him.

The choice would have been much simpler had there been no other reasonable alternative. Were I working against an imminent deadline, I would have apologized for my inability to come with him. Conversely, had I no work to do at home, and no other pressing matters, the invitation to go out with a friend would be welcome, and not reasonable to refuse. It is often the case in life that one door closes and another opens; we move from one thing to another because there is only one clear path. It is also often the case that we choose our direction not because there are no other choices, but because the other choices before us appear foolish. Any one of us could choose to quit his job, withdraw his meager savings, and travel to the holy land to await the return of Christ at the Mount of Olives, living on the street, hungry and cold but expectant. We do not do this because our view of the circumstances convinces us that it is an unreasonable course of action to take; that we need to continue in the jobs we have, supporting ourselves, possibly our families. It is for similar reasons that most of us do not quit our jobs to sell soap or vitamins door-to-door in a multi-level marketing corporation. Not to disparage those who have found success at such alternative businesses, for most of us this is not a reasonable path to take. Thus, looking at the realities of our lives through the filter of the rational logic of our God-given minds, we take paths which appear objectively correct.

Objective guidance goes beyond this. It includes the application of the moral and ethical principles which we embrace. As an example of this, there are times in our daily lives when the opportunity to acquire something which is not ours presents itself. Yet we recognize that this is wrong. Whether we perceive it in a simplistic legalistic manner, that the scripture says, "Thou shalt not steal", or whether we have grown beyond that to understand the concept that we must do to others as we would have done to us, or even if we have reached an understanding of morality which perceives that such crimes are destructive of our own personality, the fact is that we have something of an objective standard on which to base our conduct. We choose not to steal, not because at this moment we have the feeling that to do so would be wrong, but because we have the knowledge that stealing is wrong, and we can objectively perceive that it is therefore wrong to do so now. Similarly with all of our moral structure, we can articulate things which are wrong, and make choices based on that. It is part of the objective form of guidance: using reason to determine our course through circumstances.

However, there are many choices which we make which we do not consider at all. Several times a week I find myself in any one of several grocery stores. It is entirely possible that God has work for me at one of these stores, someone who needs to talk to me, something I have to do for someone. It is also possible that there is a lesson or benefit for me in one of these stores. I can remember unexpectedly stopping into a store on a bad day and running into a pastor I know, who was a great encouragement to me. Yet I don't usually give much thought to where I should be. I might stop at whichever store is closest to me, or least out of the way, or will avoid the most traffic, or will have the best price on whatever it is I need. I might go to one store and decide when I get there that it is too crowded, and go to another instead. It might even be that I will be out on another errand, see the grocery store, and stop to get something I suddenly remember needing. When I go to the grocery store, I don't often consider how it might fit into God's vast eternal plan, even though when I reflect upon the question I realize that it may well matter where I am. I don't worry about it, though, because I know that if God has some important plan for me at a particular store, I'll find myself wanting to go there.

This brings us to the subjective side of guidance.

As Christians, we know that God has come to dwell in us. He works in us to make us new creatures, and guides our lives from within. I doubt there are many who bear the name Christian who have not at some time felt that God wanted them to do something in particular—even if it was no more than repent and believe the gospel. So we all have experienced the inner "leading" of the Spirit.

Yet it is not always easy to distinguish the voice of God from those of the world, the flesh, and the devil. We learn to listen, to move, but to be ready to check our movement if anything isn't right. Many are the times when we start in a particular direction, and find "the door closed"—and then we say, "I guess that wasn't what God wanted after all."

Was it, though? Have we confused an obstacle to overcome with a closed door? How hard are we to push when things don't immediately fall into place? What tells us to give up? All of this is about balancing objective and subjective guidance—and that is the basic answer to the problem of guidance.

Let's face it, when there is only one path open, guidance is simple. Either we go that way, or we stay where we are. The objective guidance says that it is much easier to steer a vehicle which is in motion; the objective guidance says that if this is the only way, then this is the way. Thus we proceed along the only open path. However, it is possible for the subjective guidance to stop us. Some have referred to this as feeling a check in your spirit, or a warning or red light. It may be that we see only one path open, but that God tells us not to take it. This feeling that a particular path is the wrong thing is an important part of guidance.

God will not leave us standing still forever, though. If this is the wrong path, and we follow the subjective guidance to stop, we must expect that something will change. It may be that the path is the right path, but it is too soon to begin it. It may rather be that another path is about to open, and we must wait for it. If (objectively) we don't see another path soon (which

64

(subjectively) feels right), then it is likely that the check was not from God, but was from ourselves.

It is especially likely that the check comes from ourselves if the only path we see is something not wrong in itself that we personally don't want. God often will not tell us what He wants us to do as long as we have anything we are openly unwilling to do. If you are saying to God, "I'll do anything you want, as long as you don't send me as a missionary to Africa," it's very likely that God will wait for you to drop the condition. As long as there is something you will not do, God may leave only the path which appears to lead there. (The foolishness of such a position is obvious. If God wants to send you to Africa, you will not be happy anywhere else anyway, because His perfect plan must be what is best for Him, for you, and for the entire world. Besides, very few people are missionaries to foreign lands. God's plan probably begins right where you are. If you end up in Africa, you will know that there was nowhere else on earth you would rather have been.) When you see the path that leads to that which you fear, or to that which you will not accept, your own emotions will cloud your perceptions. It is important to understand that the check which tells you not to do what you don't want to do anyway might well be only your own reaction. Look for a clearer objective revelation of God's plan in that case, and drop the condition. Tell God you will do anything He asks, not "Anything but".

The opposite problem occurs when objective guidance leads to a brick wall. Suddenly the clear path becomes cloudy, the easy way becomes difficult, the open road seems to close. Many will say, "this must not be the way", but others will say, "there are obstacles to overcome". How do you determine which it is? The answer is simple: objective guidance is tempered by subjective guidance. If you're on a path because it seemed the best choice of the ways which were open, but it appears to be a dead end, of course your objective guidance will tell you that the true path lies elsewhere. However, if you are on the path that you know is the right path because God has spoken to your heart and revealed it to you, then you will see such blocks as obstacles, and begin working to move them aside.

Once again, our understanding of subjective guidance must be tempered. Especially when that which you perceive as God's intent is also that which you desire, the possibility of confusing His guidance with your desires is higher. It is certainly true that God has placed within us desires which He intends to fulfill, and that sometimes these desires will give us the motivation we need to move forward against the obstacles. It is also true that we have many wrong desires, or even right desires which we try to fulfill at the wrong time or in the wrong way. When you think your desires and God's desires are aligned, you should look for confirmation beyond the feelings you have. This will often take the form of objective guidance— the obstacle will be removed, the path will open, or a way around it will appear. It may instead or also take the form of an increased level of subjective guidance.

This is a touchy subject in the church. I can easily say that objective guidance may be clarified. Everyone will agree that if a door is open, that is a good indication that it is the right direction. All will accept the idea that if the path appears reasonable, that is better, and that if alternative paths close, there is even more reason to follow that which remains open. Further, no one will argue that if a clear moral issue is involved, this reinforces our belief that we are on the right course. Objective guidance may become stronger. When I say that subjective guidance also may become stronger, though, I risk being misunderstood. Then when I try to clarify what I mean, I run the risk of offending the beliefs of some Christians. Therefore, I must clarify with care.

I do not mean that your feelings in the matter will be stronger. This is possible, and may be an indication of God's leading in this direction. Many times we encounter obstacles which make us pause and consider, only to say, "No, I know this is what God would have me do". However, stronger feelings are often created by our own indignation, anger, or resentment at the possibility that what we want is not what God wants. I would never advise that stronger feelings themselves are a clearer or stronger sign from God that we are on the right path. If your feelings may have been wrong or confused in the first place, why should you assume that the same feelings stronger would be right? No, stronger subjective guidance goes beyond your own feelings, because subjective guidance is not really about what you feel, but about what God is trying to tell you by direct supernatural communication. If your feelings are a valid direction from God, then they represent the Holy Spirit speaking directly to your spirit. Thus any direct communication from the Spirit of God is what we are calling subjective guidance, even if it is not directly subjective to you.

Most stronger subjective guidance comes from others. Even without broaching the issue of whether there are prophets or prophetic gifts in the church today, we all realize that sometimes God gives a word of encouragement to us through a friend or pastor. This is not objective; it is still as subjective as before, but it is someone else's subjectivity. Thus when someone we know—or even someone we don't really know— tells us that they perceive that God wants us to continue in the direction we've been going, this is subjective confirmation of a higher level. This may well be God reinforcing our own feelings through the feelings of others.

This aspect of reinforcement is very important. I believe that God does tell others what He wants us to hear. However, don't believe any prophecy about what God wants for you that you haven't already heard from God. If someone surprises you with something they claim is God's will for you, you should stop and reflect as to whether God has been trying to tell you this but you've not been listening. In the end, though, God will not send someone else to tell you something He has not Himself spoken to your spirit.

This reinforcement may go beyond simple encouragement from other Christians into the realm of supernatural spiritual gifts. There may be prophetic messages; you or others may receive dreams or visions; words of wisdom or knowledge may be delivered. All of this is subjective guidance—and none of it means anything if it is not reinforcing something God is saying to you directly. God may go so far as to speak in an audible voice to you, or to someone else who may speak to you. These wonders increase the strength of subjective guidance. It is not objective guidance to receive a prophecy from another. It is a subjective reinforcement of what God is saying by His Spirit.

Christians often ask why, if God is able to provide such direct and powerful subjective guidance, He does not always do so. The answer to this becomes obvious first if we remember the many choices we constantly make. Why should God speak to you in an audible voice to tell you where to shop today? You will go where you feel you should go. Why should God tell you in a vision that you should not steal the candy from the convenience store? You have the moral sense to know this quite without such intervention. Still, the other side of the question must also be asked: if God can guide us without these extreme subjective measures, why would He ever use them? For this I will relate a story.

I have a lot of love and respect for a man I know whose ministry reaches far beyond my own. He has established a string of missions, now spreading around the world, which reach out to the lost who have destroyed their lives, especially with alcohol and drugs, but in many other ways as well. I receive his newsletter. One month it told of their efforts to open a mission in another country. It told how God had directed them to do this. There were several prophetic words delivered in their meetings, and numerous other supernatural communications supporting this. All of them felt that God wanted them to do this. Here we had subjective guidance of the highest order. They had begun the process when suddenly all of the doors slammed shut, and the government of that country staunchly opposed any further movement in that direction. The newsletter expressed some confusion that this should have happened, but I knew what happened. They should have expected trouble of this order. After all, if God wanted this man to open a mission in that country, He could have encouraged his spirit quietly in that direction, and the matter would have been settled very quickly. God knew that the road was long and hard, and there would be many obstacles. Before they put their first foot on that road He made it absolutely clear to them—subjectively, supernaturally—that this was the direction they were to take. Now they would know, when the problems came, that these were obstacles to overcome, and not God telling them not to go this way.

We find something similar in the Acts of the Apostles. After the last recorded missionary journey of Paul, he was headed back to Jerusalem with the money collected for the church there. Staying at the home of Phillip the Evangelist, he was met by the prophet Agabus. Agabus, in dramatic form, announces that Paul would be bound and imprisoned in Jerusalem, and all of the saints beg him not to go. However, Paul tells them that he knew this, that God had been telling him that he would have trouble in Jerusalem. He was ready to die there, despite the fact that he also hoped to preach in Rome—and had already written the Roman epistle telling them to expect him. Why, then, did Paul go to Jerusalem, if God told him he would be imprisoned? Are we to think that Paul disobeyed God by going to Jerusalem? If God was not telling Paul not to go, what was the point of telling him anything, or of sending Agabus?

If we look at subsequent events, we will understand. Paul did go to Jerusalem, and was falsely accused and imprisoned. He remained in prison in Jerusalem for a short time, and was then moved to Caesarea when his life was threatened. He was kept in prison there for three years.

Had I been kept in prison for three years, by the end of the first year I'm sure I would have been asking myself, "Where did I miss it? Why has God forsaken me? How did I go wrong?" For over a thousand days, Paul awoke each morning in a prison and lived a life in which he had little contact with anyone. Certainly he made the best of it, preaching the gospel to secular governors who were less likely to believe than the rocks themselves. He might have despaired. He did not. One reason he did not despair is because before it all went wrong, before this obstacle landed in his God-given path to Rome and stopped him in his tracks for three years, Agabus had come to him and told him it was going to happen. "Don't worry," God said. "There's going to be a lot of trouble on this path, but it's the right road, so keep going." In the end, of course, this road took him not merely to Rome, but right into the court of the emperor, at the expense and under the protection of the Roman government.

For most of our lives, the simple objective guidance is sufficient—we follow the path before us to wherever it leads. When the objective guidance will be misleading, though, the subjective—sometimes dramatically supernatural—guidance comes to direct us beyond this.

It is necessary to add an important footnote, a denouement, as it were. I have said that our moral and ethical principles are a part of our objective guidance. I have also said that our subjective guidance steps in when our objective guidance might mislead us. It is a logical conclusion that God could direct us to do something which we perceive as morally wrong. Further, I would be misleading you if I suggested that God has never asked anyone to do anything which that individual believed was morally wrong. Although it might not seem a moral issue to you, when God instructed Ezekiel to break the Law by eating food cooked over burning dung, to that prophet priest it was a moral issue, a direct violation of the law of God—and the law of God was no less violated when God softened it from burning human dung to burning cow's dung. I will not tell you that God will never direct you to violate your own conscience or moral principles. However, I will tell you this: any time in scripture when God commanded anyone to do anything which he perceived as immoral or morally wrong, the individual so commanded found it morally repugnant, and was not willing to do it. Expect that the same would be the case for us. God will not command you to do something which you believe is wrong but wanted to do anyway. If He commands you to do something you believe is wrong, it will also be something you find personally difficult and offensive. The only exception to this would be when God is trying to teach you that your laws are not His—much as the vision given to Peter, when that apostle needed to understand that gentiles were not unclean, that you have made rules for yourself which He did not give—and in that case, it will still be something you did not wish to do. God will not command you to commit the sin to which you are sorely tempted.

Ultimately, Christian conduct is about what God wants you to do right now. Thus guidance is an essential part of knowing how to live the Christian life. Hopefully, finding that Christian path will be easier with these tools. It is not always simple, and we are not always completely certain of our course. We may be certain, however, that God is directing us as long as we are willing to follow Him.

Notes and Afterword

This journey began with the assertion that a gospel-based approach to Christian conduct could not be couched in the kinds of rules that say what we should and should not do, that Christianity was not about replacing the Ten Commandments with either a more demanding Law or a more lenient one. It has carried us through concepts that should guide our conduct. We act from love, love guided by knowledge. That knowledge comes as we renew our minds, seeing as God sees. This wisdom teaches us to do what is best for us and for others, to embrace our freedom while shielding ourselves and our brothers from temptation. Ultimately we must discover our own gifts, the good things God has placed within each of us, and discover how to use these in the service of others, as we follow His leading through our minds and spirits to know what He would have us do. In one sense, that's all there is to it. In another, that is the work of a lifetime.

It would not be possible to thank or mention everyone who has contributed to this short book; the formation of my understanding of the gospel has owed so much to so many.

Some of this material is more or less similar to articles previously published on the Internet. The chapter on guidance has undergone only minor revision from an earlier web page version, and the Parable of the Boiler has been copied nearly intact. Material on Philemon and weaker brothers has also been published before, with much the same substance although here in a new form. It was compiled roughly into this book sometime around 2002, but for various reasons was lost, found, and revised for this release.

The Secret was written in 1976, and also appeared on the Internet in the late 1990s.

I must credit Dr. John Herzog for the analogy between salvation and the British royal family. Jay E. Adams' insights

72

into I Corinthians 10:13 were invaluable. To anyone else who sees their impact on my thought uncredited, I apologize for the oversight. My gratitude extends to pastors, teachers, authors, evangelists, musicians, fellow Christians, family members, friends, and complete strangers who have in one way or another helped me find my direction and my place in this body, and I cannot even remember, let alone name, all.

It is my earnest expectation and hope that this book will be of some small assistance in understanding the road to which we are called, and that those read it would find it worth recommending to others who struggle to understand the outworking of this faith of ours. It always encourages me to hear that something I wrote benefited someone. Thank you for taking the time to read and consider these thoughts.

—Mark Joseph Young

About the Author

M. Joseph Young has been involved in various ministries through music, broadcasting, teaching, and the Internet, since the early 1970's. Currently Chaplain of the Christian Gamers Guild, he brings to his work an understanding of Christianity not fettered by particular denominational bounds. His broad background includes degrees in Biblical Studies from Luther College of the Bible and Liberal Arts (an arm of Lutheran Bible Ministries) and Gordon College, and a doctorate from Widener University School of Law. He has authored several other published books, including the novel Verse Three, Chapter One.

Additional Books by the Author:

Do You Trust Me?
A fresh examination of what faith is, and why it has always been the basis of salvation.

Why I Believe
A detailed examination of why many intelligent people believe in Jesus.

The Essential Guide to Time Travel
A consideration of the various theories of the nature of time.